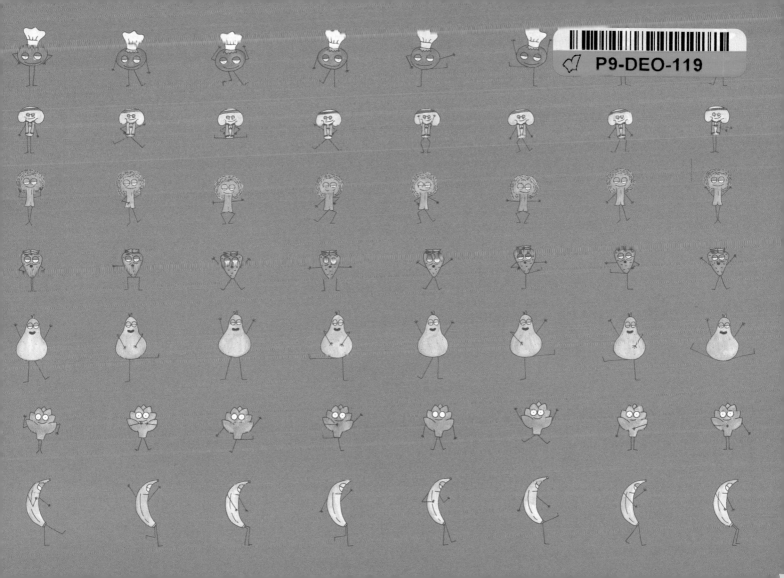

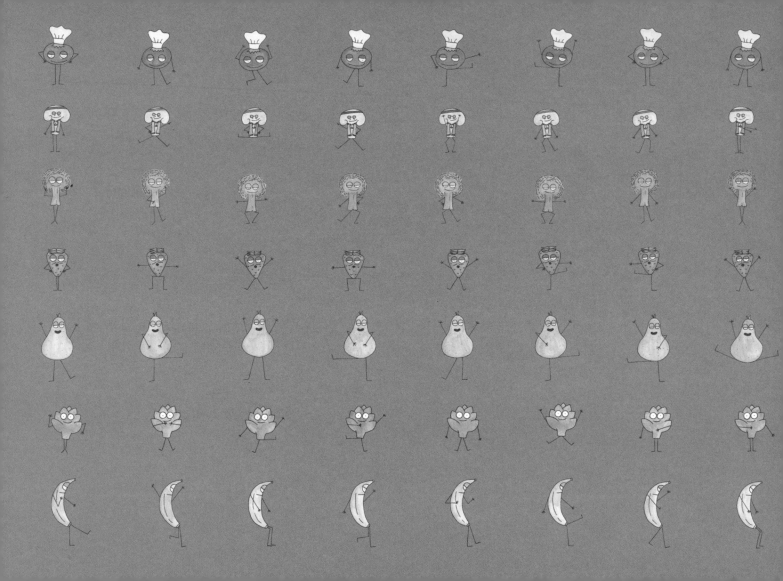

The Vegan Stoner

Cookbook

The Vegan Stoner

TEN SPEED PRESS
Berkeley

Published in the United States by Ten Speed Press,
an imprint of the Crown Publishing Group,
a division of Random House, Inc., New York.
www.crownpublishing.com   www.tenspeed.com

Ten Speed Press and the Ten Speed Press colophon
are registered trademarks of Random House, Inc.

Some of these recipes originally appeared on the
authors' website, TheVeganStoner.com.

Design by S\G Design Studio

Library of Congress Cataloging-in-Publication Data
Conrique, Sarah.
  The vegan stoner cookbook : 100 easy vegan recipes
to munch / Sarah Conrique and Graham I. Haynes.
    pages cm
  Includes index.
1. Vegan cooking. I. Haynes, Graham I. II. Title.
  TX837.C5973 2013
  641.5'636—dc23
              2013005503
ISBN 978-1-60774-464-1   eISBN 978-1-60774-465-8

Printed in China

10

First Edition

Figgy

Keep the Grass Green

Paper

Glass

Legend

○ Large Portions

○ Small Portions

121 Helpful Reference

25 Ideal Munching Time and Page Number

Marché Local

✕ munch

Dead man's Crossing

Melon Beach

Tools Required

Spoon

Fork

Knife

Cup

Bowl

Blender

Pan

Hands

Pot

Pipe (Optional)

Baking Sheet

INTRODUCTION

ve·gan ston·er [vee-guhn stoh-ner] — noun: one who satisfies the munchies with resourceful, creative, instinctive cooking without using animal products.

These recipes are designed to make vegan cooking fun, feasible, quick, and on a dime. Each recipe—for a sauce, a stuffing, or a base –is a potential component in your personal munchie menu. Mix and match with confidence. Substitute ingredients and flavors to personalize dishes for you, for two, or for a party. Explore the depths of your creativity.

There will be moments when you will be in doubt. Trust yourself, dig in with your fingers, and grab what feels right. Pay attention to consistency, texture, smell, and, most importantly, your taste buds. In time you will rely less on exact measurements and more on instinct.

Don't be afraid to go where no one in your kitchen has gone before. Cook for yourself, and know that the only success in cooking is when you have fun.

The Vegan Stoner

Breakfast

3

Biscuits and Gravy

Serves ◯◯ or ◯◯◯

Tips

- Add more creamer if gravy is too thick.
- Use gravy as sauce for mashed potatoes or Holiday Pie 66.

☆ Monsieur Moonshine's
CRESCENT ROLL DOUGH

VEGGIE CHURNER
VEGGIE DOGS

Spice Chest
BASIL

Spice Bowl
GARLIC SALT

THIRSTY BEAN
SOY CREAMER

ANGRY WHEAT
WHOLE WHEAT FLOUR

Criminal Caps
CRIMINI MUSHROOMS

1
Unroll crescent dough and cut out circles with a cup.

2
Toss dough circles on a baking sheet, then bake according to package.

3
Chop a handful of shrooms, ¼ onion, and a vegan dog.

4
Cook chopped ingredients in an oiled pan.

5
Add 1 cup soy creamer to pan with ¼ cup flour, a sprinkling of basil, and a sprinkling of garlic salt.

6
Lower heat and stir till thick, then pour over stacked biscuits.

7
Munch.

Breakfast Pizza

Serves ◯◯ or ◯◯◯

Tips

- To make pizza for 4 to 6 people, use all of dough and double other ingredients.
- Try pesto, marinara 105, or Mac and Peas sauce 32 instead of ketchup.

1
Preheat oven to 375°F.

2
Roll out ½ of dough on an oiled baking sheet and bake for 10 min.

3
Chop ½ bell pepper, 2 cloves of garlic, and a handful of broccoli.

4
Mix ½ block of tofu and a handful of nutritional yeast in a bowl.

5
Remove dough from oven and layer with ketchup, tofu, and veggies.

6
Sprinkle with Creole 102 and bake for 10 more min.

7
Munch.

Date Shake

Serves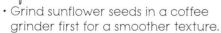

Tips
- Grind sunflower seeds in a coffee grinder first for a smoother texture.
- Add an apple or other fruits.
- Add cocoa powder or agave for a dessert shake.

SUNFLOWER SEEDS

Soy High

SOY MILK

1
Toss a handful of dates in a blender.

2
Add a banana, a handful of sunflower seeds, and 1 cup soy milk.

3
Blend.

4
Munch.

Fresh Baked Granola

 Serves ◯ ◯ ◯

Tips
- Add protein powder for a boost.
- Dip bars in melted chocolate for a candy bar.
- Replace maple syrup with agave or molasses.

1
Preheat oven to 350°F.

2
Melt ½ cup peanut butter in a pan with ½ cup maple syrup.

3
Mix in ¼ cup applesauce, 3 cups oats, and 1 cup trail mix.

4
Spread in an oiled baking pan and bake till brown, about 30 min.

5
Cut into bars or crush to make clusters.

6
Munch.

Fried Tofu and Waffles

Serves ⚪⚪ or ⚪⚪⚪

Tips

- To cut down sweetness, coat tofu in veggie oil instead of syrup in step 3.
- Use fried tofu in a sandwich with veggies and veganaise 107.

1
Slice ½ block of tofu into thick rectangles.

2
Mix 2 handfuls of bread crumbs with a sprinkling of Creole 102 in a bowl.

3
Coat tofu in syrup, then in bread crumb mixture.

4
Heat ¼ cup oil in a pan and fry both sides of tofu till brown.

5
Toast waffles and top with tofu, fruit, and syrup.

6
Munch.

Granola Bowl

Serves  or

Tip

• Add your favorite combination of frozen fruit and/or fresh fruit.

PEANUT BUTTER

FROZEN BERRIES

OATS AND GOATS GRANOLA

ORANGE JUICE

Soy High
SOY MILK

1
Toss 1 cup frozen berries in a blender.

2
Add a banana and a sliced apple.

3
Add a scoop of peanut butter.

4
Add 1 cup orange juice and 1 cup soy milk.

5
Blend, pour, and add a handful of granola.

6
Munch.

Hollandaise Benedict

Serves ◯◯ or ◯◯◯

Tips

- Add turmeric to sauce for a brighter yellow color.
- Thin sauce with soy milk.
- Use sauce as a cheese replacement in other recipes.

1
Heat ¼ cup vegan sour cream in a pan.

2
Stir in a handful of nutritional yeast and a few sprinklings of garlic salt, then set sauce aside to thicken.

3
Slice tofu, then cut out circles with a cup.

4
Cook both sides of tofu in an oiled pan till brown.

5
Slice a tomato and an avocado.

6
Toast English muffins and layer all ingredients on top.

7
Munch.

Jam Danishes

Serves ⬤⬤ or ◯◯◯

Tips

- Skip step 3 and seal rectangles together for a quick version.
- For a savory version, skip step 6 and try cooked veggies with soy cream cheese instead.
- Use marinara [105] soy cheese, and veggies for a pocket pizza.

PUFF PASTRY DOUGH

SOY CREAM CHEESE

Strawberry Top
JAM

POWDERED SUGAR

Soy High
SOY MILK

VANILLA EXTRACT

1
Preheat oven to 400°F and thaw pastry dough [106].

2
Cut dough into rectangles, then cut holes out of centers of half of them with a cup.

3
Stack dough rectangles with holes on top of dough without holes. Place on a baking sheet.

4
Bake for 10 min. Scoop 2 spoonfuls of vegan cream cheese into each center.

5
Bake for 5 more min. Scoop a spoonful of jam into each center.

6
Mix 4 spoonfuls of powdered sugar, a spoonful of soy milk, and a splash of vanilla in a bowl, then drizzle onto Danishes.

7
Munch.

Mean Green Smoothie

Serves or

Tips
- Add cilantro or celery.
- Top with granola and fresh-cut fruit.

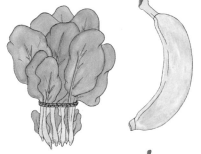

1
Toss a handful of frozen peas, a banana, and a sliced pear in a blender.

2
Add a handful of kale and 2 handfuls of spinach leaves.

3
Add ½ cup coconut milk and ½ cup water.

4
Blend.

5
Munch.

Ohmlette

Serves ◯ or ◯◯

Tips

- Serve with ketchup or chili sauce.
- Use a muffin pan to make mini portions.
- Layer other cooked veggies between tofu mixture for a hidden surprise.

SOFT TOFU

TURMERIC

YELLOW YETI'S NUTRITIONAL YEAST

THIRSTY BEAN SOY CREAMER

GARLIC SALT

Soy High CHEDDAR SOY CHEESE

Criminal Caps CRIMINI MUSHROOMS

1
Preheat oven to 375°F.

2
Blend ½ block of tofu in a blender with a handful of nutritional yeast, a sprinkling of turmeric, and ½ cup soy creamer till smooth.

3
Chop a handful of spinach and mix it in with a sprinkling of garlic salt.

4
Pour mixture into an oiled pie pan and bake for 15 min.

5
Slice a handful of shrooms.

6
Remove pan from oven, then top with a handful of soy cheese and shrooms.

7
Bake for 10 min. Fold in half.

8
Munch.

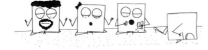

13

Orange French Toast

Serves ◯ or ◯◯

Tips
- Using stale bread instead of fresh helps to soak in flavor.
- Add 1 to 2 spoonfuls of flour to juice mixture for a gooier batter.
- Try coconut oil in place of margarine.

SOY MILK

ORANGE JUICE

CINNAMON

MARGARINE

MAPLE SYRUP

POWDERED SUGAR

1
Mix ½ glass of soy milk and ½ glass of orange juice in a bowl.

2
Mix in 1 spoonful of cinnamon and 2 spoonfuls of powdered sugar.

3
Melt a spoonful of margarine in a pan.

4
Slice bread, dip each slice in juice mixture, then cook both sides in a pan till brown.

5
Serve with syrup and powdered sugar.

6
Munch.

Peachy Crêpes

Serves  or

Tips

- If you use fresh fruit instead of canned, replace peach syrup in step 2 with soy milk.
- For a dinner crêpe, replace fruit with cooked veggies and peach syrup with soy milk, and top with vegan cream cheese.

ANGRY WHEAT
WHOLE WHEAT FLOUR

SoyHigh
SOY MILK

oily toasts
MARGARINE

Keeping it Together Co.
SLICED PEACHES

Queen Cane's
POWDERED SUGAR

happy trees
MAPLE SYRUP

1
Mash a banana in a bowl with 1 cup soy milk.

2
Mix in 1 cup flour, 2 spoonfuls of melted margarine, and ¼ cup peach syrup drained from can.

3
Pour ¼ cup of batter into a hot oiled pan.

4
Spread batter into a thin circle and lower heat.

5
Flip crêpe over when bubbles appear and bottom browns.

6
Place peach slices in middle of crêpe and roll.

7
Repeat till batter is gone, then top with syrup and powdered sugar.

8
Munch.

Tofu English Muffin

FIRM TOFU

Samurai's Soy Sauce

YELLOW YETI'S NUTRITIONAL YEAST

MOZZARELLA SOY CHEESE

oily toast's MARGARINE

TEA TIME MUFFINS
ENGLISH MUFFINS

Serves ◯◯ or ◯◯◯

Tips
- Try a mix of your favorite veggies.
- Replace soy cheese with hollandaise [10].

1
Cut a block of tofu into squares. Slice a zucchini into coins.

2
Coat tofu in soy sauce then nutritional yeast.

3
Melt a spoonful of margarine in a pan.

4
Fry both sides of tofu and zucchini.

5
Melt vegan cheese on top of mixture in pan.

6
Pile all ingredients on toasted English muffins.

7
Munch.

Yam Scramble

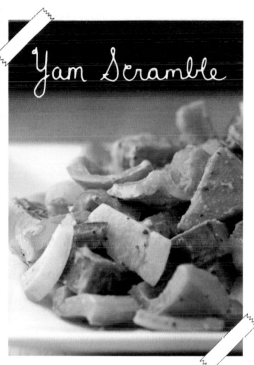

Serves or ○○

Tips

- Add chopped jalapeño, cumin, or curry powder 102 for extra flavor.
- Replace yam with eggplant and a splash of soy sauce.
- Roll into warm tortilla for a breakfast wrap.

1
Chop ½ yam, ¼ onion, and a green bell pepper.

2
Cook chopped veggies in a covered pan with ½ cup water till soft, about 12 min.

3
Mix in a handful of nutritional yeast, a sprinkling of adobo 102, and a spoonful of mustard.

4
Munch.

Aspara-Guy Sushi

Serves

Tips

- Serve with soy sauce or your favorite dipping sauce.
- Replace veggies and rice with your favorite veggies and grains.

SUSHI RICE

SALT

RICE VINEGAR

Candy Man's SUGAR

ORGANIC NORI SHEETS

Sea Weed's

1
Cook 1 cup dry sushi rice in a pot 114.

2
Mix in 3 spoonfuls of rice vinegar, 2 spoonfuls of sugar, and a few sprinklings of salt.

3
Trim ends off a handful of asparagus, wrap in a wet paper towel, and microwave till soft.

4
Slice asparagus, a carrot, and ½ avocado into long slivers.

5
Spread a thin layer of rice on rough side of a nori sheet, then add a few slices of veggies in middle.

6
Firmly roll nori from one end to the other like a sleeping bag and seal with water 113.

7
Slice, then repeat steps 5 and 6.

8
Munch.

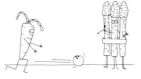

Bahnwich

Serves ◯ or ◯◯

Tips

- Replace seitan with Soy Curls.
- Serve prepared ingredients over salad greens instead of bread for a lighter version.

NEWTON'S GLUTEN

SEITAN

YAY-NAY VEGANAISE

CHILI SAUCE

CONFUSED CONFUSIVE HOISIN SAUCE

Well-Bread FRENCH ROLLS

Angry Grapes BALSAMIC VINEGAR

1
Slice a carrot and ½ cucumber.

2
Coat sliced veggies with balsamic vinegar in a bowl, then set aside.

3
Slice a handful of seitan, boil in water for 5 min., then drain.

4
Cook seitan in a pot with 2 spoonfuls of hoisin sauce till brown, then set aside.

5
Mix a spoonful of veganaise [107] with a spoonful of chili sauce in a bowl.

6
Spread veganaise sauce on toasted bread, then layer on seitan and sliced veggies.

7
Munch.

Baked Lentil Potato

Serves ◯ or ◯◯

Tip
- Replace toppings with chives,
  gravy ④, and vegan sour cream ⑩⑦.

The Gentle Lentil

LENTIL SOUP

¡PEPPER VILLA'S!

SALSA

Criminal Caps'

CRIMINI MUSHROOMS

1
Poke holes in 2 potatoes with a fork, wrap in a wet paper towel, and microwave till soft ⑪⑪.

2
Empty a can of lentil soup into a pot and heat.

3
Slice a handful of shrooms and add to pot.

4
Split open potatoes and pour soup on top.

5
Top with salsa.

6
Munch.

Carnitacos

Serves ◯ or ◯◯

Tips

- Add cooked veggies and legumes for a heartier version.
- Top with vegan sour cream 107 and hot sauce.
- Replace seitan with Soy Curls for a different texture.

NEWTON'S GLUTEN

SEITAN

Samurai's Soy Sauce

Chili's CHILI SAUCE

Señor Pescado CORN TORTILLAS

Spice tub ADOBO

1
Slice a handful of seitan, boil in water for 5 min., and drain.

2
Chop a tomato and ¼ onion.

3
Cook seitan in a pan with a spoonful of soy sauce, a spoonful of chili sauce, and a sprinkling of adobo 102.

4
Mix juice from ½ lime into pan.

5
Heat tortillas, then layer on veggies and seitan.

6
Munch.

Collard Wraps

Serves ◯ or ◯◯

Tips

- Add chopped tomatoes and cooked rice for a heartier version.
- Bake collard wraps in a baking pan topped with your favorite sauce.

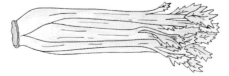

SUNFLOWER SEEDS

SOY MILK

SEED SMUGGLER TAHINI

BLACK OLIVES

GARLIC SALT

1
Toss 1 cup sunflower seeds, ½ cup soy milk, 2 spoonfuls of tahini [103], and a sprinkling of garlic salt in a blender.

2
Blend.

3
Chop 2 stalks of celery and a handful of olives.

4
Mix olives and celery into sunflower seed mixture.

5
Scoop mixture into collard leaves and roll.

6
Munch.

Corn Chowder

Serves or

Tips

- Add vegan sausage for a heartier version.
- Serve with crackers or add tortilla chips and hot sauce for a quick tortilla soup.

1
Wrap ½ potato in a wet paper towel and microwave till soft 111.

2
Chop cooked potato, ¼ onion, and a handful of spinach.

3
Heat potato, onion, and spinach in a pot with ½ cup veggie broth.

4
Mix in ½ can drained corn, ½ cup soy creamer, a spoonful of flour, and a sprinkling of Creole 102.

5
Lower heat and stir till thick.

6
Munch.

Cran-Yam Bowl

Serves

Tips

- Toss everything in a tortilla with legumes for a quick wrap.
- Flavor with hoisin sauce instead of soy sauce.

BROWN RICE

Super Grains Co.

Samurai's Soy Sauce

Smokey's LIQUID SMOKE

In Pieces Co.
CHOPPED BROCCOLI

Deserted Cran's
DRIED CRANBERRIES

1

Cook 1 cup dry rice in a pot [114].

2

Poke holes in a yam, wrap in a wet paper towel, and microwave till soft [111].

3

Chop yam.

4

Cook yam in an oiled pan with 2 handfuls of chopped broccoli, a handful of cranberries, a spoonful of soy sauce, and a few drops of liquid smoke.

5

Serve over rice.

6

Munch.

Cream of Shroom Soup

Serves 🥣 or 🥣🥣

Tips

- Add more soy milk or veggie broth if soup gets too thick.
- Add a few more spoonfuls of flour to make a thick gravy.

CRITICAL CAPS
CRIMINI MUSHROOMS

oily toast's
MARGARINE

Soy High
SOY MILK

FALLING VEGGIES
VEGGIE BROTH

Samurai's Soy Sauce

ANGRY WHEAT
WHOLE WHEAT FLOUR

Spice Cap
CUMIN

Spice tote
THYME

1
Slice 2 handfuls of shrooms and a few stalks of kale.

2
Cook shrooms in a pot with a spoonful of margarine and 2 spoonfuls of soy sauce.

3
Add 1 cup soy milk, ½ cup veggie broth, and a spoonful of flour.

4
Mix in a sprinkling of cumin, a sprinkling of thyme, and chopped kale.

5
Lower heat and stir till kale wilts.

6
Munch.

Curry Dog

Serves ◯ or ◯◯

Tips

- Serve dog and curry over rice or baked on pizza dough.
- Replace curry mixture with your favorite sauce.

1
Skin a mango and chop into chunks.

2
Cook mango chunks in an oiled pan.

3
Mix in ¼ cup coconut milk, a spoonful of chili sauce, a sprinkling of cumin, and a sprinkling of curry powder 102 .

4
Set aside curry and cook a vegan dog in oiled pan.

5
Toast a bun, then place dog inside.

6
Top with mango curry and chopped green onion.

7
Munch.

Eggplant Sandwich

Serves ⬤⬤ or ◯◯◯

Tips

- Serve cooked veggie mix over rice with your favorite sauce.
- Replace veganaise with vegan cheese and sandwich between 2 tortillas.

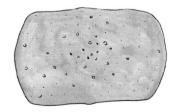

1
Chop a tomato, ½ eggplant, and a handful of olives.

2
Cook eggplant in an oiled pan with 2 spoonfuls of balsamic vinegar and a sprinkling of garlic salt.

3
Mix tomato and olives into pan and cook till eggplant darkens.

4
Spread veganaise 107 on toasted bread and layer veggies on top.

5
Munch.

Fried Tofu Tacos

Serves ◯◯ or ◯◯◯

Tips
- Add a squeeze of lime juice and a sprinkling of Creole [102] for flavor.
- Use fried tofu in a sandwich with veganaise mixture and some veggies.

CHILI SAUCE

FIRM TOFU

SOUR CREAM

Samurai's Soy Sauce

SHREDDED CABBAGE

PANKO CRUMBS

CORN TORTILLAS

1
Mix 2 spoonfuls of vegan sour cream with a spoonful of chili sauce in a bowl.

2
Heat 5 small tortillas and spread sour cream mixture on top.

3
Layer a handful of cabbage strips onto tacos.

4
Slice ½ block of tofu into rectangles.

5
Coat tofu in soy sauce, then panko crumbs.

6
Coat a pan with oil, fry tofu on both sides, and layer onto tacos.

7
Munch.

Lentil Burger

Serves

Tips

- Replace lentils with your favorite legumes.
- When shaping patties, stuff vegan cheese and chives into center.
- Shape patties into logs for a vegan dog replacement.

1
Cook ½ cup dry lentils in a pot [115].

2
Chop ¼ onion and slice ½ tomato.

3
Mix cooked lentils in a bowl with onion, 1 cup oats, and ¼ cup veggie broth.

4
Shape lentil mixture into patties with wet hands.

5
Coat a pan with oil and fry patties on both sides.

6
Place patties on buns with veganaise [107], sliced tomatoes, and a handful of sprouts.

7
Munch.

31

Mac and Peas

Serves   or ...

Tips

- Let sit for 10 min. to make thicker.
- Add fresh veggies, garlic, hummus, or tahini 103 .

MACARENA MAC — MACARONI

Chili's — CHILI SAUCE

YELLOW YETI'S — NUTRITIONAL YEAST

Bees and Peas — PEAS

ANGRY WHEAT — WHOLE WHEAT FLOUR

YODELING SEED — MUSTARD

oily toasts — MARGARINE

1

Cook 1 cup dry pasta in a pot according to package.

2

Melt 2 spoonfuls of margarine in a pan.

3

Add ½ cup water and a can of drained peas.

4

Mix in a handful of nutritional yeast and 2 handfuls of flour.

5

Mix in a spoonful of mustard and a spoonful of chili sauce.

6

Mix cooked pasta into sauce.

7

Munch.

Philly Sandwich

Tips

- Place in a pita bread for a quick wrap, or in a tortilla for a quesadilla.
- Replace bread with pasta, and soy cheese with your favorite sauce for a new dish.

NEWTON'S GLUTEN

SEITAN

Soy Thrive Co.

MOZZARELLA SOY CHEESE

Criminal Caps'

CRIMINI MUSHROOMS

Well-Bread

FRENCH ROLLS

YAY-NAY VEGANAISE

1
Slice a handful of shrooms, ½ bell pepper, and ¼ onion into strips.

2
Chop 2 garlic cloves and toss in a pan with a spoonful of veganaise 107.

3
Slice a handful of seitan and add to pan with all sliced veggies.

4
Mix in a handful of soy cheese and cook till melted.

5
Spoon onto toasted bread.

6
Munch.

Portobello Island Burger

Serves ◯◯

Tip
• Chop veggies and fruit and serve over rice for a teriyaki stir-fry.

1
Marinate 2 portobello tops for at least 5 min. in equal amounts of teriyaki sauce and pineapple juice drained from can.

2
Cook shrooms in an oiled pan with a few slices of onion and a splash of teriyaki sauce.

3
Toast 2 burger buns and spread with veganaise 107.

4
Stack red cabbage leaves, pineapple, shrooms, and sliced onions on buns.

5
Munch.

Shredded Papaya Salad

Serves ◯ or ◯◯

Tip
- Add chopped tofu or seitan for a heartier version.

LAZY GRINGO CO. GREEN BEANS

Samurai's Soy Sauce

Marching Peanuts Co. PEANUTS

Spice drawer CHILI FLAKES

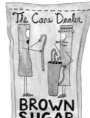
The Cane Dealer BROWN SUGAR

1
Chop 2 garlic cloves, a handful of peanuts, and a handful of green beans.

2
Toss in a bowl with a spoonful of chili flakes, a handful of brown sugar, a splash of soy sauce, and juice from 1 lime.

3
Shred outer skin of a green papaya and stir into bowl.

4
Munch.

Sloppy Janes

Serves

Tips

- Replace bread with tortillas and replace barbecue sauce with salsa for a quick taco mix.
- Add lentils and oats to thicken mixture for burgers or "neatloaf."

Seedy Inn

VACANCY

BURGER BUNS

VEGGIE GYMS'
TVP
textured vegetable protein

Colonel Beans'

BBQ SAUCE

1
Chop ½ bell pepper and ¼ onion.

2
Boil 1 cup of water in a pot.

3
Mix in chopped veggies and 1 cup dry TVP.

4
Pour in ½ cup barbecue sauce.

5
Serve on bread buns.

6
Munch.

Spinach Shroom Streudel

Serves ◯ or ◯◯

Tips.
- Use a pastry brush if you have one for steps 3 through 6.
- For streudel filling, use your favorite veggies, vegan cheese, or sauce.
- Replace veggies with fruit or jam to make a phyllo Danish.

SOY CREAM CHEESE

MARGARINE

PHYLLO DOUGH

CRIMINI MUSHROOMS

1
Thaw phyllo dough and preheat oven to 375°F.

2
Chop a handful of shrooms, 3 garlic cloves, and 3 handfuls of spinach. Cook in an oiled pan with 3 spoonfuls of soy cream cheese.

3
Melt 2 spoonfuls of margarine and spread thinly on a sheet of dough.

4
Top sheet of dough with a second sheet plus margarine. Repeat for 4 or 5 layers.

5
Spoon half of veggie mix onto center of dough and fold all ends over middle to form a square.

6
Brush with margarine, press, and seal closed

7
Bake for 15 min., slice, and serve.

8
Munch.

Split Pea Soup

Serves 🥣 or 🥣🥣

Tip
- Drain out liquids and mash solids for a hearty stuffing for tacos or wraps, or add to curries and more.

SPLIT PERSONALIPEAS'
SPLIT PEAS

BLACK PEPPER

CAYENNE

Samurai's Soy Sauce

FROZEN VEGETABLES

FALLING VEGGIES
VEGGIE BROTH

NEWTON'S GLUTEN
SEITAN

1
Cook 1 cup of dry split peas in 1 cup water and 2 cups veggie broth in a pot till soft.

2
Chop ¼ onion and add to pot with 1 cup frozen veggies.

3
Chop a handful of seitan and cook in a pan with 2 spoonfuls of soy sauce till brown.

4
Pour soup into bowls and top each with seitan, a sprinkling of black pepper, and a sprinkling of cayenne.

5
Munch.

TVP Salad

Serves 🥣 or 🥣🥣

Tips

- Use as stuffing for sushi or rice balls, or serve on buns as a light Sloppy Jane.
- Place on collard greens for a wrap.
- Replace TVP with cooked legumes.

1
Chop a carrot, 2 stalks of celery, 2 garlic cloves, and ¼ onion.

2
Boil 1 cup water in a pot, then stir in 1 cup dry TVP.

3
Remove pot from heat and mix in chopped veggies.

4
Mix in 3 spoonfuls of veganaise [107] and a spoonful of soy sauce.

5
Munch.

Bagel Dogs

Serves

Tips

- Replace vegan dogs with a legume patty for a bagel burger.
- Roll ingredients in a tortilla.

1
Slice 2 vegan dogs lengthwise and cook in an oiled pan.

2
Slice a bagel in half and stack vegan cheese on top.

3
Microwave bagel till cheese melts.

4
Layer ketchup, mustard, kraut, and cooked dogs on bagel slices.

5
Munch.

Banana Dog

Serves ◯

Tip
- Mash all ingredients and use as a stuffing mixture for enchiladas or taquitos.

1
Peel a banana.

2
Chop ¼ onion.

3
Cook onion and banana in a pan with a spoonful of veggie oil and a sprinkling of Creole [102].

4
Mix 2 spoonfuls of veganaise [107] with a sprinkling of cumin in a bowl.

5
Spread veganaise mixture on a toasted bun, then add banana and onion.

6
Top with ketchup.

7
Munch.

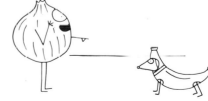

Black Bean Dip

Serves or

Tips

- Use dip in burritos, tacos, wraps, and sandwiches.
- Layer in a large dish with vegan sour cream 107, guacamole, vegan cheese, and salsa for a layered dip to share.

1
Toss a can of drained black beans in a blender.

2
Blend with ¼ cup salsa, 2 spoonfuls veganaise 107, a sprinkling of cumin, and a sprinkling of cayenne.

3
Serve with tortilla chips and chopped avocado.

4
Munch.

Chili Cheese Fries

Serves or ◯◯

Tips

- Replace potato with veggies like zucchini, carrot, or yam.
- Skip potatoes and use chili and cheese sauce on a vegan dog, sloppy joe, or layered dip.

1
Preheat oven to 400°F.

2
Slice a potato into wedges, coat with olive oil, and place on a baking sheet.

3
Sprinkle wedges with adobo [102] and bake for 10 min.

4
Flip wedges over and sprinkle with more adobo. Bake 10 more min.

5
Heat ½ can of chili and set aside.

6
Heat 2 handfuls of nutritional yeast in a pot with ½ cup soy creamer, a sprinkling of adobo, 2 spoonfuls tahini [103], and a spoonful of olive oil.

7
Pile everything together.

8
Munch.

Chive Pancake

Serves

Tip
· Mix chili sauce into soy sauce for a spicier dip.

1
Chop a handful of chives and about 3 green onions.

2
Mix 1 cup flour, 1 cup water, and ¼ cup soy yogurt in a bowl.

3
Cook a handful of chopped veggies in an oiled pan with a sprinkling of garlic salt.

4
Pour batter on top of veggies in a circular pattern 110.

5
Flip when bottom browns, then repeat steps 3 to 5.

6
Serve with soy sauce.

7
Munch.

Croquettes

ADOBO

FROZEN VEGETABLES

KIDNEY SWAP

KIDNEY BEANS

Sensei Toast's
PANKO CRUMBS

Serves ◯ ◯

Tips
- Skip breading and baking and serve with gravy [4].
- Replace potatoes with a mash of your favorite legume.

1
Preheat oven to 400°F.

2
Poke holes in 2 potatoes with a fork, wrap each in a wet paper towel, and microwave till soft [111].

3
Mash potatoes in a bowl with a few sprinklings of adobo [102].

4
Chop ½ onion and cook in an oiled pan with a handful of frozen veggies and ½ can of kidney beans.

5
Mix veggies into potatoes, then shape mixture into patties.

6
Coat patties in panko crumbs and bake for 30 min. on a baking sheet.

7
Munch.

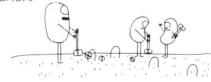

Deviled Lentils

Serves or

Tips

- Top with gravy [4] or your favorite sauce.
- Stuff potatoes with your favorite legumes.
- Mix in some relish in step 4.

1

Cook ¼ cup of dry lentils in a pot [115].

2

Slice a potato into 4 pieces, cover with a wet paper towel, and microwave till soft [111].

3

Scoop out a hole in middle of each potato piece.

4

Mash cooked lentils with a spoonful of veganaise [107], 2 spoonfuls of mustard, a sprinkling of Creole [102], and scooped-out potato.

5

Microwave a handful of frozen veggies according to package and stir into lentil mixture.

6

Scoop lentil mixture into potato holes.

7

Munch.

Dill-Weed Sandwich

Serves ◯ or ◯◯

Tip
· Serve on crackers for a quick bite-sized snack to share with a group.

1
Slice 2 garlic cloves, 1 tomato, and ½ cucumber.

2
Mix garlic slices with 3 spoonfuls of veganaise [107] and a sprinkling of dill in a bowl.

3
Spread veganaise mixture on toasted bread.

4
Layer tomato slices and cucumbers on toasted bread.

5
Sprinkle with salt.

6
Munch.

Enchilada Rolls

Serves ⬤⬤ or ◯◯◯

Tip
- Try marinara sauce instead of enchilada sauce.

Monsieur Moonshine's
CRESCENT ROLL DOUGH

NEWTON'S GLUTEN
SEITAN

Soy High
CHEDDAR SOY CHEESE

Pepé y Lupé's
ENCHILADA SAUCE

1
Preheat oven to 375°F.

2
Cut dough into triangles.

3
Stack sliced seitan and soy cheese on dough.

4
Roll up dough and place on a baking sheet.

5
Bake according to package, about 10 min.

6
Slice ½ avocado and use as a topping with enchilada sauce.

7
Munch.

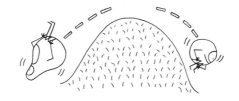

Lucky Lettuce Wraps

Serves  or ◯◯

Tips

- Serve over brown rice instead of noodles and lettuce.
- For a quick chow mein, double sauce, and cook in pan with noodles.

POOF!
INSTANT NOODLES

CONFUSED CONFUCIUS'
HOISIN SAUCE

TEMPTING
TEMPEH

NUTTY NUTS
CASHEWS

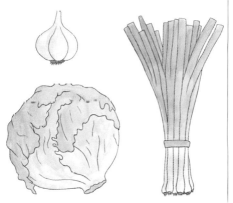

1
Cook a package of instant noodles, drain, and set aside.

2
Chop 2 garlic cloves, 2 green onions, 2 handfuls of tempeh, and a handful of cashews.

3
Cook chopped garlic in an oiled pan.

4
Mix in chopped tempeh, cashews, green onions, and 2 spoonfuls of hoisin sauce.

5
Serve on lettuce with noodles.

6
Munch.

Miso Stuffing

Serves

Tips

- Replace miso soup with your favorite instant soup.
- Use miso paste instead of instant mix for a richer soup.

1
Prepare 1 cup of instant miso soup.

2
Chop 5 cups of stale bread and soak in a bowl with miso soup.

3
Chop 2 stalks of celery, 3 handfuls of shrooms, and ½ onion.

4
Melt a spoonful of margarine in a pan and cook chopped veggies with a sprinkling of rosemary.

5
Mix in bread and a sprinkling of adobo 102.

6
Munch.

Pizza Bread

Serves  or

Tips
- Use different veggies.
- Make a double recipe for a great party hors d'oeuvre.
- Use carrot sauce 62 instead of marinara.

1
Preheat oven to 400°F.

2
Microwave 3 spoonfuls of margarine in a bowl till melted.

3
Slice ½ baguette and dip each slice in margarine.

4
Cover bottom of a baking pan with bread slices.

5
Slice 3 garlic cloves and a handful of shrooms.

6
Top bread with garlic, shrooms, a handful of spinach leaves, and marinara 105.

7
Bake for 10 min.

8
Munch.

Samosas

Serves or

Tips

- Try fresh seasonal veggies instead of frozen ones.
- Replace potato with your favorite legume.

PUFF PASTRY DOUGH

CURRY POWDER

FROZEN VEGETABLES

GARLIC SALT

1
Thaw pastry dough and preheat oven to 400°F.

2
Chop a potato and boil in a pot of water with 2 handfuls of frozen veggies till soft.

3
Drain and mash together with a spoonful of curry powder 102 and a sprinkling of garlic salt.

4
Cut dough into squares.

5
Form each square into a cone in one hand, then spoon veggie mix into center 113.

6
Fold and seal each end closed, then bake on an oiled baking sheet for 30 min.

7
Munch.

Shepherd Dumplings

Serves ◯◯ or ◯◯◯

Tip
• Bread and fry dumplings for a crispy shell.

1
Heat ½ can of lentil soup in a pot, then add a handful of frozen veggies.

2
Mix in a handful of dry TVP, then set aside.

3
Cook 4 servings of instant mashed potatoes according to package, mixing in a sprinkling of adobo [102].

4
Form potato mixture into a ball, then flatten in palms.

5
Scoop a spoonful of soup mixture into center.

6
Press outer edges together to form a cup, then sprinkle with black pepper.

7
Munch.

Shroom Ceviché

Serves ◡ or ◡◡

Tips

- Add avocado and legumes for a quick taco, enchilada, or burrito stuffing.
- Blend with chili sauce or peppers for an easy salsa.

CHERRY TOMATOES

GARLIC SALT

Blue and Yellow

TORTILLA CHIPS

1
Chop a portobello, ¼ onion, and a handful of cherry tomatoes.

2
Cook shroom in a pan with a splash of water.

3
Drain and toss in a bowl with cherry tomatoes.

4
Mix in onion, a few sprinklings of garlic salt, a handful of cilantro, and juice from 3 limes.

5
Serve with chips.

6
Munch.

Spring Rolls

FIRM TOFU

COCONUT MILK

PEANUT BUTTER

CRIMINI MUSHROOMS

HOISIN SAUCE

RICE PAPER

 Serves ◯ ◯

Tips
- Replace stuffing with tempeh mixture from Lucky Lettuce Wraps 51.
- For a dessert spring roll, replace veggies with fruit and serve with a sweetened soy yogurt dip.

1
Slice a tomato, ½ block of tofu, and a handful of shrooms into strips.

2
Run water over both sides of rice paper.

3
Stack a handful of basil leaves, tofu, tomato, and shroom strips in middle of rice paper.

4
Fold top and bottom of rice paper in, roll closed from left to right, and seal with water 113.

5
Repeat steps 2 to 4.

6
For dipping sauce, mix a spoonful of melted peanut butter, 2 spoonfuls of hoisin, and 3 spoonfuls of coconut milk in a bowl.

7
Munch.

Tempeh Tacos

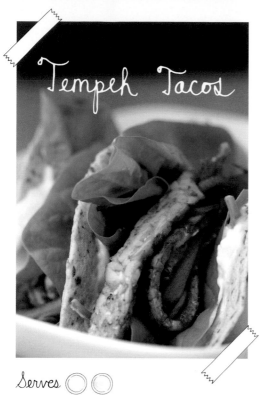

Serves ○○

Tips

- Add soy cheese or mashed legumes and sandwich between 2 tortillas for a quesadilla.
- Replace tortillas with bread for a yummy sandwich.

YAY-NAY VEGANAISE

Señor Pescado's FLOUR TORTILLAS

CONFUSED CONFUCIUS' HOISIN SAUCE

1
Slice a handful of tempeh.

2
Cook tempeh in an oiled pan with 2 spoonfuls of hoisin.

3
Heat 4 small tortillas.

4
Spread veganaise 107 on tortillas and top with spinach and tempeh.

5
Munch.

Tofu Puff Pastry

Serves

Tips

- Top with your favorite veggies.
- Try sealing stuffing between 2 sheets of pastry dough for a handheld pocket.
- Use topping for a pizza.

PUFF PASTRY DOUGH

SOFT TOFU

Samurai's SOY SAUCE

NUTRITIONAL YEAST

CHERRY TOMATOES

1
Preheat oven to 400°F and thaw pastry dough 106.

2
Mash ½ block of tofu.

3
Chop a jalapeño and ¼ onion.

4
Mix tofu and veggies in a bowl with a spoonful of lime juice, 2 spoonfuls of soy sauce, and a handful of nutritional yeast

5
Cut dough into rectangles and bake on a baking sheet for 10 min.

6
Remove from oven, spread tofu mixture on top, and bake for 10 more min.

7
Remove and top with cherry tomatoes.

8
Munch.

Dinner

61

Carrot Pizza

Serves ⬭⬭ or ⬭⬭⬭

Tips
- Layer toppings on toasted bread slices for a decadent garlic bread.
- Use toasted pita bread for dough.
- Use chopped spinach instead of carrot tops.

1
Preheat oven to 375°F, roll out half of premade dough on an oiled baking sheet, and bake for 10 min.

2
Chop 2 carrots and their tops, ¼ onion, and 2 garlic cloves.

3
Cook carrot bottoms in a pan with a splash of water till soft.

4
Toss cooked carrots in a blender with ¼ cup soy creamer and ¼ cup olive juice drained from can to make a sauce.

5
Cook carrot tops in pan with chopped garlic and a splash of water.

6
Layer carrot sauce on dough with carrot tops, onion, and a handful of sliced olives. Bake for 10 more min.

7
Munch.

Chickpea Curry

Tips
- Serve over vegan dogs instead of rice.
- Replace chickpeas with your favorite legume or protein.

BROWN RICE

COCONUT YOGURT

CHICKPEAS

CURRY POWDER

GARLIC SALT

1
Cook ½ cup of dry rice in a pot [114].

2
Chop a carrot and a bell pepper.

3
Cook a can of drained chickpeas, 1 cup coconut yogurt, and chopped veggies in a pot till soft.

4
Mix in a spoonful of curry powder [102] and a sprinkling of garlic salt.

5
Serve on cooked rice.

6
Munch.

Corned Seitan Hash

Serves ◯ ◯

Tip
• Replace potato with your favorite legume or try it in a sandwich.

1
Chop a potato, a carrot, 2 handfuls of cabbage, and a handful of seitan.

2
Cook chopped potato and veggies in an oiled pan till soft.

3
Mix in a few sprinklings of garlic salt and pour mixture in a bowl.

4
Cook seitan in pan with a spoonful of mustard and add to bowl.

5
Munch.

Falafel Pie

 Serves ◯ ◯ ◯ ◯

Tips
- Works well in a pie pan or muffin tray.
- Add your favorite falafel toppings.
- Stuff into collards or add a layer of pita bread.

1
Preheat oven to 350°F.

2
Mix 1 cup of falafel mix with ½ cup of water.

3
Spread falafel mix in an oiled baking pan and bake till brown, about 15 min.

4
Remove from oven and top with a thick layer of hummus.

5
Slice a tomato and ½ cucumber, then layer on pie.

6
Blend a cup of soy yogurt, a spoonful of lemon juice, and ½ cucumber in a blender.

7
Pour mixture on pie and top with a handful of olives.

8
Munch.

Holiday Pie

Serves

Tips

- Add chopped vegan dogs for a heartier version.
- Add your favorite veggies or a layer of cranberry sauce in middle.
- Top with gravy [4].

SOY MILK

INSTANT STUFFING

CRIMINI MUSHROOMS

SOFT TOFU

Samurai's SOY SAUCE

1
Preheat oven to 425°F.

2
Make stuffing according to package and spread 2 cups into a pie pan.

3
Chop a handful of shrooms and 3 garlic cloves.

4
Cook shrooms and garlic in an oiled pan with 2 spoonfuls of soy sauce, then set aside.

5
Blend a block of tofu and ½ cup soy milk in a blender.

6
Stir shrooms and garlic into tofu mixture.

7
Pour mixture into pie pan and bake for 30 min.

8
Munch.

Lasagna

Serves ○ ○ ○ ○

Tip

- Replace marinara with your favorite sauce.

1

Preheat oven to 350°F.

2

Boil 12 lasagna noodles in a pot, then drain.

3

Chop 3 stalks of kale, a handful of shrooms, and a small squash.

4

Cover bottom of a baking pan with marinara 105 and a layer of lasagna noodles

5

Add layers of squash, kale, shrooms, sauce, and more noodles.

6

Mash 3 scoops of soy cream cheese, ½ block of tofu, and a handful of nutritional yeast in a bowl, then spread in baking pan.

7

Add a layer of noodles, top with sauce, and bake uncovered for 40 min.

8

Munch.

Lentil Loaf

Serves

Tips

- Substitute fresh seasonal vegetables for frozen veggies.
- Try barbecue sauce instead of ketchup.

THREE LEGUMES'
LENTILS

FAT WALRUS Co

WALNUTS

FROZEN VEGETABLES

Everything
CRACKERS
We have everything seeds too!

Chef Stoner's
TOMATO KETCHUP

MRS. CRABBY APPLE'S
APPLESAUCE

Spice bowl
GARLIC SALT

1
Preheat oven to 350°F.

2
Cook a cup of dry lentils in a pot 115.

3
Chop ½ onion and a handful of walnuts.

4
Mash cooked lentils with onion, walnuts, and 2 handfuls of crushed crackers.

5
Mix in a sprinkling of garlic salt, 2 cups frozen veggies, 4 spoonfuls of applesauce, and 2 spoonfuls of ketchup.

6
Pack into a baking pan and top with ketchup.

7
Bake till firm, about 40 min.

8
Munch.

Pad Thai

Serves

Tips
- Replace noodles with shredded papaya and green beans for a healthier version.
- Try serving on lettuce for a quick wrap.

BEAN SPROUTS

AGAVE

INSTANT NOODLES

CHILI SAUCE

NEWTON'S GLUTEN

SEITAN

Samurai's Soy Sauce

1
Cook 2 servings of instant noodles according to package, then set aside.

2
Chop a handful of seitan and cook in an oiled pan with a spoonful of soy sauce.

3
Add cooked noodles, 2 spoonfuls of chili sauce, and a handful of bean sprouts to pan.

4
Mix in 2 spoonfuls of soy sauce, a spoonful of agave, and juice from ½ lime.

5
Munch.

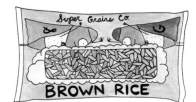

Peanut Stew

Serves ◯◯

Tips
- Add shrooms or garlic.
- Replace tomatoes with bell peppers, or potatoes with cauliflower.

BROWN RICE

PEANUT BUTTER

THYME

CHICKPEAS

STEWED TOMATOES

1
Cook 1 cup dry rice in a pot 114.

2
Chop a potato, wrap in a wet paper towel, and microwave till soft 111.

3
Chop ½ onion and cook in an oiled pot.

4
Add potato, 1 can of stewed tomatoes, ½ cup crunchy peanut butter, ½ can of chickpeas, and a sprinkling of thyme.

5
Cover pot, lower heat, and cook for 20 min.

6
Serve over rice.

7
Munch.

Polenta Peppers

Serves ◯ ◯

Tips

- Add leafy greens or your favorite veggies in step 3.
- Bake polenta, sauce, and veggies in a baking pan for a casserole to share.

MOZZARELLA SOY CHEESE

MARINARA

ADOBO

POLENTA

1

Slice ¼ tube of polenta and a poblano pepper.

2

Cook both sides of polenta in an oiled pan with a sprinkling of adobo [102] till brown, then toss on a plate.

3

Cook sliced pepper in an oiled pan till dark green.

4

Add 1 cup marinara [105], a handful of soy cheese, juice from a lime wedge, and a sprinkling of adobo.

5

Pour mixture on top of polenta.

6

Munch.

Potatoes Au Gratin

Serves ◯ ◯ ◯ ◯

Tips

- Top with marinara [105], ketchup, or soy cheese.
- Use garlic salt if you don't have fresh garlic.

1
Preheat oven to 400°F.

2
Slice 2 potatoes and 3 garlic cloves.

3
Toss a can of drained beans in a bowl.

4
Mash beans with chopped garlic, 1 cup soy milk, ¼ cup tahini [103], 2 spoonfuls of mustard, and a couple sprinklings of thyme.

5
Layer bean mixture and potatoes in an oiled baking pan till ingredients are gone.

6
Crumble a slice of bread on top, cover, and bake for 40 min.

7
Munch.

Potato Hash

Serves ⊙⊙ or ⊙⊙⊙

Tips

- Serve over rice, biscuits, or English muffins.
- Use your favorite legumes in place of potato.
- Try adding your favorite veggies.

NEWTON'S GLUTEN

SEITAN

ANGRY WHEAT

WHOLE WHEAT FLOUR

oily toasts

MARGARINE

Spice Pail

SALT

THIRSTY BEAN

SOY CREAMER

1
Poke holes in a potato with fork, wrap in a wet paper towel, and microwave till soft ⏲.

2
Chop potato, a carrot, and a handful of seitan.

3
Cook chopped veggies in a pot with 2 spoonfuls of margarine.

4
Mix in seitan, ¾ cup soy creamer, a spoonful of flour, and a sprinkling of salt.

5
Cover pot and cook till thick.

6
Munch.

Pumpkin Casserole

Serves ○○○○

Tips
- Replace pumpkin mixture with marinara [105] or your favorite sauce.
- Use sunflower topping on Mac and Peas [32].

PENNE PASTA

YELLOW YETI'S NUTRITIONAL YEAST

PUMPKIN PURÉE

SUNFLOWER SEEDS

GARLIC SALT

1
Preheat oven to 400°F.

2
Boil 2 cups dry pasta, drain, then spread in an oiled baking pan.

3
Cook a can of pumpkin purée in an oiled pan with a handful of nutritional yeast and a few sprinklings of garlic salt.

4
Layer mixture into baking pan.

5
Slice a zucchini and layer it into baking pan.

6
Chop 2 garlic cloves and 1 cup sunflower seeds.

7
Mix together with a sprinkling of garlic salt and layer on top of casserole.

8
Bake for 30 min.

9
Munch.

Pumpking Enchiladas

Serves ◯ ◯

Tips

- Replace seitan with Soy Curls.
- Replace pumpkin mixture with your favorite stuffings, or replace enchilada sauce with your favorite sauce.

FLOUR TORTILLAS
Señor Pescado's

Scared Squash
PUMPKIN PURÉE

Pepé y Lupé's
ENCHILADA SAUCE

YELLOW YETI'S
NUTRITIONAL YEAST

NEWTON'S GLUTEN
SEITAN

Spice pot
CREOLE SEASONING

YODELING SEED
MUSTARD

1
Chop a handful of seitan, boil in water for 5 min., then drain.

2
Chop ¼ onion.

3
Cook half of chopped onions in an oiled pan with seitan and a spoonful of mustard.

4
Mix in a few spoonfuls of enchilada sauce, ½ can of pumpkin purée, 3 spoonfuls of nutritional yeast, and a sprinkling of Creole [102].

5
Wrap mixture in tortillas.

6
Heat tortillas with rest of chopped onions in oiled pan.

7
Coat with enchilada sauce.

8
Munch.

Quiche

Serves ◯ ◯ ◯ ◯

Tips

- Use a muffin tray for individual portions.
- Add your favorite mix of veggies or a layer of cranberry sauce in middle for holidays.

1
Preheat oven to 425°F.

2
Chop ½ onion, a handful of shrooms, and 2 cups of broccoli.

3
Cook veggies in an oiled pan.

4
Blend a block of tofu and ½ cup soy milk in a blender.

5
Mix everything in bowl with a sprinkling of curry powder [102] and a spoonful of garlic salt.

6
Pour into premade pie crust and bake for 40 min.

7
Munch.

Seitan Stroganoff

Serves

Tip
• Serve over rice instead of noodles.

1
Boil 2 servings of noodles in a pot, then drain.

2
Slice a handful of shrooms and a handful of seitan into strips.

3
Slice ½ onion and cook in a pot with a spoonful of margarine.

4
Mix in shrooms, seitan, and ½ cup vegan sour cream.

5
Mix in a sprinkling of salt, a spoonful of parsley, and a spoonful of flour.

6
Stir till thick and serve over noodles.

7
Munch.

Southern Bowl

Serves ◯ ◯

Tip
• Replace rice with your favorite grain.

BROWN RICE

PECANS

CORN

BBQ SAUCE

BLACK EYED PEAS

1
Cook ½ cup dry rice in a pot [114].

2
Poke holes in a yam with fork, wrap in a wet paper towel, and microwave till soft [111].

3
Chop yam, 3 collard leaves, and a handful of pecans.

4
Cook ½ cup of black-eyed peas and ½ cup corn in an oiled pan.

5
Add yam and pecans to pan with ¼ cup barbecue sauce.

6
Add greens and stir till wilted.

7
Serve over rice.

8
Munch.

Stuffed Cannelloni

Serves ⬭⬭

Tip
- Add your favorite cooked veggies to stuffing mixture and replace marinara with your favorite sauce.

1
Boil 6 cannelloni pasta shells, then drain.

2
Mix ¼ cup falafel mix and ¼ cup water in a bowl.

3
Chop a handful of walnuts and a handful of basil, then add to bowl.

4
Mix in ½ block of tofu and a spoonful of soy cream cheese.

5
Stuff cannelloni shells with falafel mixture.

6
Top with marinara 105 and cook in an oiled pan.

7
Munch.

Swedish Neatballs

Serves

Tips
- Try serving neatballs over shredded veggies or pasta.
- Use this sauce in other recipes.

VEGGIE BROTH

MEATLESS MEATBALLS

PLAIN SOY YOGURT

YODELING SEED
MUSTARD

ADOBO

Samurai's Soy Sauce

BASIL

1
Microwave 2 handfuls of frozen meatless meatballs according to package.

2
Heat balls in an oiled pan with 5 spoonfuls of soy yogurt.

3
Add 2 spoonfuls of soy sauce, 2 spoonfuls of veggie broth, and a sprinkling of adobo [102].

4
Mix in a sprinkling of basil and a spoonful of mustard.

5
Serve over a handful of spinach.

6
Munch.

Tempeh and Chips

Serves ◯◯

Tips
- Serve with vinegar or ketchup.
- Try fried tempeh in a sandwich.

1
Mix a handful of cornmeal, ½ cup flour, and ½ cup water in a bowl.

2
Mix in a handful of panko crumbs, a sprinkling of Creole 102, and juice from ½ lemon.

3
Slice 2 handfuls of tempeh and dip both sides in batter.

4
Heat ¼ cup oil in a pan and fry tempeh on both sides.

5
Cook frozen French fries according to package and serve with tempeh.

6
Munch.

Yakisoba

Serves

Tips

- Add tempeh or your favorite protein.
- Serve on lettuce for a quick wrap.

INSTANT NOODLES

GINGER

Samurai's Soy Sauce

Seed Smuggler
SESAME SEEDS

EDAMAME FISHING EDAMAME
FROZEN EDAMAME

CONFUSED CONFUCIUS'
HOISIN SAUCE

1
Cook a package of instant noodles according to package, then set aside.

2
Slice 2 carrots and 2 garlic cloves.

3
Cook carrots and ½ cup bagged edamame with ¼ cup water in a covered pan till soft.

4
Add chopped garlic, noodles, and 2 spoonfuls of hoisin.

5
Mix in 2 spoonfuls of soy sauce and a sprinkling of ginger.

6
Top with a sprinkling of sesame seeds.

7
Munch.

Zucchini Beanballs

Serves ◯◯

Tips

- Any type of legume will work.
- Turn beanballs over gently while frying so they don't fall apart.

1
Slice 2 zucchinis into long strips and cook in an oiled pan with 2 spoonfuls of soy sauce.

2
Mash ½ can of drained black beans in a bowl with a handful oats and 2 spoonfuls soy sauce.

3
Roll bean mixture into balls and coat with bread crumbs.

4
Fry beanballs in pan with ¼ cup oil, then set aside.

5
Heat about 1 cup marinara 105, then combine all ingredients.

6
Munch.

85

Animal Cookies

Serves ◯◯

Tip
• Add a splash of beet juice for a colorful, natural pink version.

ANIMAL CRACKERS

THIRSTY BEAN
SOY CREAMER

Queen Cane's
POWDERED SUGAR

Leaky Cones'
VANILLA EXTRACT

'oily toasts'
MARGARINE

Confetti Marts
SPRINKLES

1
Microwave a spoonful of margarine till melted.

2
Mix melted margarine with ½ cup powdered sugar, 2 spoonfuls of soy creamer, and a splash of vanilla.

3
Mix in 2 more spoonfuls of powdered sugar.

4
Dip crackers in mixture and lay on a nonstick baking sheet.

5
Top with sprinkles and place in freezer till solid.

6
Munch.

Apple-Rice Pudding

Serves  ◯ ◯

Tip
- Replace apple with your favorite fruit, or raisins with your favorite dried fruit.

BROWN RICE

COCONUT MILK

Old Grapes'
RAISINS

Spice Can
CINNAMON

Candy Man's
SUGAR

1
Cook ½ cup dry rice in a pot [114].

2
Stir in ¼ cup coconut milk,
2 handfuls of raisins, and
2 spoonfuls of sugar.

3
Chop an apple and add to pot.

4
Sprinkle cinnamon on top.

5
Munch.

Baked Banana Cake

Serves

Tip

- Use your favorite fruit or make a multilayered version with mixed fruit.

oily toasts'
MARGARINE

Candy Man's
SUGAR

Leaky Cones'
VANILLA EXTRACT

COCONUT MILK

1
Preheat oven to 350°F.

2
Slice 2 bananas and toss in a bowl with a handful of sugar, then set aside.

3
Heat 1 cup coconut milk in a pot with a handful of sugar and a splash of vanilla.

4
Soak 4 slices of bread in pot with coconut milk.

5
Layer banana slices and soaked bread in an oiled baking pan till all ingredients are gone. Drizzle a spoonful of melted margarine on top.

6
Cover pan with foil and bake for 30 min.

7
Munch.

SWIRLIE'S ICE CREAM

Carrot Muffins

Serves ○ ○ ○ ○

Tips
- Replace carrots with zucchini
- Bake in a cake pan for a special occasion.

1
Preheat oven to 350°F.

2
Make cake batter according to package, with vegan substitutions 109. Set aside.

3
Melt ¼ cup margarine and blend in a blender with 3 carrots, a banana, and 1 cup of water.

4
Mix carrot mixture with cake mix, a spoonful of cinnamon, and 2 handfuls of raisins.

5
Pour batter into an oiled cupcake pan and bake for 25 min.

6
Remove from oven and top with soy cream cheese, cinnamon, and chopped walnuts.

7
Munch.

Chocolate Mousse

 Serves 🥣🥣

 Tip

- Replace cocoa powder with vanilla extract, dates, or fresh strawberries.

1
Melt 2 cups chocolate chips in microwave for 1 min., stir, and toss in a blender.

2
Blend with a block of tofu, 3 spoonfuls of soy creamer, and 2 spoonfuls of cocoa powder.

3
Mix 2 handfuls of fruit and a spoonful of agave in a bowl.

4
Layer a handful of crumbled cookies, chocolate mixture, and fruit into 2 cups.

5
Microwave a handful of chocolate chips till melted, mix with a splash of soy creamer, and drizzle over mousse.

6
Munch.

Churro Chips

Serves ◯◯

Tip
• Thicker, chewier tortillas make better churro chips.

SUGAR

CINNAMON

CORN GUY CO.

VEGETABLE OIL

Señor Pescado's

FLOUR TORTILLAS

Puddle Jumper

VANILLA PUDDING MIX

Soy High

SOY MILK

1
Preheat oven to 400°F.

2
Mix 2 spoonfuls of cinnamon and 2 handfuls of sugar in a bowl.

3
Slice 2 tortillas into small triangles.

4
Coat both sides of tortilla slices in veggie oil, then sugar mixture.

5
Bake on a baking sheet for 5 min.

6
Mix 1 cup soy milk with 1 package pudding mix for a dip.

7
Munch.

Coconut Macaroons

Serves

Tip
• Add dried fruit and nuts.

1
Preheat oven to 350°F.

2
Mix a handful of sugar, 3 handfuls of shredded coconut, and a handful of flour in a bowl.

3
Add ¼ cup soy milk and a splash of vanilla.

4
Mix and shape into balls.

5
Bake on an oiled baking sheet for 10 min.

6
Microwave a handful of chocolate chips in a bowl till melted.

7
Remove macaroons from oven and dip in melted chocolate.

8
Munch.

Easy Pumpkin Pie

Serves

Tip
- Replace pumpkin with your favorite fruit purée.

GRAHAM CRACKER CRUST

PEANUT BUTTER

CINNAMON

AGAVE

PUMPKIN PURÉE

FAT WALRUS Co

WALNUTS

COCONUT MILK

1
Toss ½ can of pumpkin purée in a blender.

2
Blend with a handful of dates, 3 spoonfuls of peanut butter, ½ cup coconut milk, 2 spoonfuls of agave, and a sprinkling of cinnamon.

3
Crumble pieces of graham cracker pie crust and layer them into 2 bowls.

4
Pour pumpkin mixture into bowls and sprinkle chopped walnuts on top.

5
Munch.

Fruit Tortilla Wraps

Serves  ◯ ◯

Tips
- Drizzle with melted chocolate.
- Use your favorite fruits.
- Replace peanut butter with vegan cream cheese.

Berry Baron's
STRAWBERRIES

Nut Butt Co.
PEANUT BUTTER

Señor Pescado's
FLOUR TORTILLAS

agave guy co
AGAVE

1
Chop a banana, a handful of strawberries, and ½ apple.

2
Spread peanut butter on 2 tortillas.

3
Layer fruit on peanut butter with a drizzle of agave.

4
Sandwich one tortilla on top of other tortilla.

5
Heat both sides of tortillas in an oiled pan till brown.

6
Munch.

Mango Sherbet

Serves

Tips
- Use your favorite fruits.
- Mix in chunks of fruit for extra flavor.

1
Peel and chop a mango.

2
Toss in a blender with a handful of sugar and juice from ½ lime.

3
Blend and pour into a freezer-safe bowl.

4
Blend 2 handfuls of frozen raspberries with ½ cup of soy creamer.

5
Swirl into bowl and freeze.

6
Serve when hardened.

7
Munch.

Mochi Sandwiches

Serves

 Tip
• Mix in your favorite nuts, dried fruit, or fresh fruit for a new flavor.

 RICE FLOUR

 COCONUT MILK

THE COOKIE EXCHANGE
VANILLA COOKIES

Candy Man's
SUGAR

Big Chips
CHOCOLATE CHIPS

1
Mix ½ cup rice flour with ½ cup coconut milk and ¼ cup water in a bowl.

2
Cover and microwave for 1 min.

3
Uncover, mix well, then microwave again for 2 min.

4
Boil ¼ cup coconut milk in a pot with ½ cup sugar till it dissolves.

5
Combine both mixtures and cool.

6
Sandwich mixture between cookies and freeze for 15 min.

7
Microwave a handful of chocolate chips and mix in 2 spoonfuls of coconut milk.

8
Dip frozen cookies in fudge.

9
Munch.

Monkey Bread

Serves

Tip

- Substitute crescent dough with puff pastry dough or fill muffin trays for mini cinnamon cupcakes to share.

Monsieur Moonshine's
CRESCENT ROLL DOUGH

Old Grapes'
RAISINS

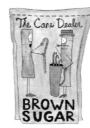
The Cane Dealer
BROWN SUGAR

Wilderness Mans'
PECANS

Queen Cane's
POWDERED SUGAR

Oily toasts'
MARGARINE

Sappy Tree
MAPLE SYRUP

Spice Can
CINNAMON

1
Preheat oven to 375°F.

2
Melt 2 spoonfuls of margarine in a bowl. Mix in 3 spoonfuls of brown sugar, a spoonful of cinnamon, and a handful of raisins.

3
Layer half of dough in a small baking dish and bake for 10 min.

4
Remove from oven and layer raisin mixture on top.

5
Add another layer of dough and bake for 16 min.

6
Mix 2 spoonfuls of powdered sugar in bowl with a spoonful of maple syrup and a handful of chopped pecans.

7
Spread maple icing on bread.

8
Munch.

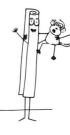

Pancookie

Serves ○ ○

Tip

· Add chopped nuts or oats for heartier pancookies.

Baked Antoinette
CAKE MIX

Conry's Island
SOY ICE CREAM

Big Chip's
CHOCOLATE CHIPS

Berry Baron's
STRAWBERRIES

1
Mix cake batter according to package, with vegan substitutions 109.

2
Mix in a handful of chocolate chips.

3
Pour ¼ cup of batter into a hot oiled pan and flip when it starts to bubble.

4
Remove when brown and repeat till batter is gone.

5
Top pancookies with strawberries and vegan ice cream.

6
Munch.

Peanut Butter Squares

Serves ○○○○

Tip
• Try using chunky peanut butter.

1
Microwave ½ bag of chocolate chips in a bowl till melted.

2
Pour into a baking pan and freeze, about 30 min.

3
Mix ½ cup peanut butter with a handful of powdered sugar in a bowl.

4
Spread peanut butter mixture on frozen chocolate.

5
Microwave rest of chocolate chips till melted and spread on top.

6
Freeze for about 1 hour.

7
Munch.

Adobo Seasoning

1

Mix a spoonful of onion powder, a spoonful of garlic powder, and a spoonful of black pepper in a bowl.

2

Mix in a sprinkling of chili powder, a sprinkling of dried oregano, a sprinkling of cumin, and 3 spoonfuls of salt.

3

Funnel into bottle and store for up to a year.

Creole Seasoning

1

Mix a spoonful of black pepper, a spoonful of onion powder, a spoonful of cayenne, a spoonful of dried oregano, and a spoonful of dried thyme in a bowl.

2

Mix in 2 spoonfuls of paprika, 2 spoonfuls of salt, and 2 spoonfuls of garlic powder.

3

Funnel into bottle and store for up to a year.

Curry Powder

1

Mix 3 spoonfuls of paprika, a few sprinklings of cumin, and a few sprinklings of cayenne in a bowl.

2

Mix in a spoonful of coriander, a spoonful of turmeric, and a sprinkling of cinnamon.

3

Funnel into bottle and store for up to a year.

Almond Milk

Makes 4 Cups

1
Soak 2 cups of unsalted almonds in water overnight, then drain.

2
Blend almonds with 4 cups fresh water in a blender.

3
Strain blended mixture through cheesecloth into a container.

4
Store in fridge for up to a week.

Tahini

Makes 2 Cups

1
Toast 2 cups of sesame seeds in an oiled pan till they start to brown. Let cool.

2
Blend seeds in a blender with ¼ cup olive oil.

3
Cook uncovered on low heat for 1 hour.

4
Store in fridge for up to 3 months.

Herb Oil

Makes 2 Cups

Tips

• Grind herb with coffee grinder before step 2.
• Use to replace oil in any recipe.
• Use sparingly at first to test potency, less than 1 spoonful per person.

1
Fill a medium pot halfway with water.

2
Add 1 cup of herb and cook on low for 1 hour.

3
Add 2 cups coconut oil and cook till melted.

4
Remove from heat and cool overnight to 3 days at room temperature.

5
Reheat on low for an hour and strain into a second pot.

6
Refrigerate till oil hardens on top of water.

7
Remove hardened oil from water and toss out water.

8
Melt oil in a pan, pour into a glass jar, and store for up to a year in fridge.

Marinara Sauce

Makes 3 Cups

Tips

- Add sliced shrooms and a chopped vegan dog in step 4.
- Add fresh hot peppers for a spicy marinara.

1
Chop ¼ onion, 1 garlic clove, 1 stalk of celery, and ½ carrot.

2
Cook chopped onion and garlic in a pot with ¼ cup olive oil.

3
Add chopped celery and carrot, then cook till soft.

4
Add 4 chopped tomatoes and a few sprinklings of salt and pepper.

5
Lower heat and cook uncovered for 1 hour.

6
Store in fridge for up to a week.

Pastry Dough

Makes 10" x 14" Slab

1
Mix 1 cup flour with a few sprinklings of salt in a bowl.

2
Mix in 1 cup crumbled margarine and ½ cup water, then cover and place in fridge for 20 min.

3
Roll out dough on floured surface, fold, then roll out again.

4
Cover and place in fridge for at least 20 more min. before using.

Tortillas

Makes 8 Tortillas

1
Mix 2 cups flour with a sprinkling of salt and 3 spoonfuls of olive oil in a bowl.

2
Mix in 1 cup water, knead, then divide dough into eight balls.

3
Roll each ball into a thin circle on a floured surface.

4
Cook both sides in an oiled pan till brown.

Veganaise

Makes 1 Cup

1
Toss ½ cup soy milk in a blender with 1 cup veggie oil, a spoonful of agave, and a spoonful of vinegar.

2
Blend.

3
Mix in a squeeze of lemon and a sprinkling of salt.

4
Store in fridge for up to 2 weeks.

Vegan Sour Cream

Makes 1 Cup

1
Toss a block of tofu in a blender with 3 spoonfuls of olive oil and juice from ½ lemon.

2
Blend with ¼ cup soymilk and a sprinkling of salt.

3
Store in fridge for up to a week.

Veggie Broth

Makes 8 Cups

1

Chop 4 garlic cloves, 1 onion, 2 stalks of celery, and a carrot.

2

Fill a large pot with 8 cups water and chopped veggies.

3

Add a handful of shrooms and a handful of spinach.

4

Add a crushed tomato and simmer uncovered for about an hour.

5

Mix in a sprinkling of salt and pepper.

6

Strain broth into a container.

7

Store in fridge for up to 2 weeks.

A Guide to Vegan Stoner Measurements

 Spoonful = 1 tablespoon

 Handful = ¼ cup

 Sprinkling = pinch to ¼ teaspoon

 Squeeze = 1 teaspoon

 Splash = 2 tablespoons

Vegan Substitutions

1 Egg

½ banana
¼ cup applesauce or fruit purée
¼ cup blended soft tofu
1 spoonful ground flax seeds + 3 spoonfuls water
1 spoonful cornstarch + 3 spoonfuls water

Milk

Almond milk
Coconut milk
Hemp milk
Oat milk
Soy milk

Butter

Coconut oil
Margarine (without casein)
Olive oil
Safflower oil
Vegetable oil

Meat

Legumes
Seitan
Tempeh
Tofu
TVP (Textured Vegetable Protein)

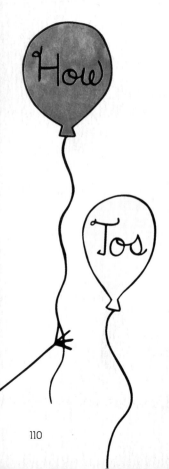

How to Cook Crêpes and Pancakes

1
Heat a splash of oil or cooking spray in a pan over high heat.

2
Wet your fingers with water and splash water into pan till it sizzles.

3
Pour ¼ cup of batter into center of pan and sprinkle any toppings.

4
Use spoon to even out mixture in a circular motion, then lower heat to medium.

5
Wait until bubbles pop up on surface.

6
Gently slide spatula underneath and loosen edges from pan.

7
Move spatula to center, quickly lift up, and flip over.

8
Remove when both sides are brown.

9
Repeat steps 1 to 8 till mixture is gone.

How to Cook on a Stovetop

1

Add a spoonful of veggie oil to a pan, then tilt to spread oil across bottom.

2

Heat over a burner set to medium to medium-high heat.

3

Add chopped food and stir.

4

Look for doneness cues:
For onions, till translucent.
For other veggies, till tender.
For tofu, seitan, and polenta, till brown.

Tip

· Preheat oil first before adding food to prevent excess oiliness.

How to Fry

1

Add a splash of high-heat veggie oil to a pan, tilt to spread across bottom.

2

Heat over a burner set to medium-high heat.

3

Wet fingers and splash water in pan till it sizzles.

4

Add food to pan.

5

Flip when bottom is brown.

6

Cook till other side is brown.

7

Lay food on paper towel.

How to Microwave Yams and Potatoes

1

Rinse in water.

2

Poke holes in surface with a fork.

3

Wrap in a wet paper towel and place on a microwave-safe plate.

4

Microwave on high for 4 min.

5

Turn over and microwave till soft, 2 to 5 min.

How to Microwave a Squash

1
Rinse squash.

2
Slice in half lengthwise.

3
Scoop out seeds.

4
Add splash of water to a microwave-safe dish.

5
Lay one side of squash on dish, face down.

6
Microwave on high for 3 min., then check softness.

7
Repeat step 6 till squash is soft.

How to Roll Burritos

1
Spread mushy mixtures first in center of tortilla.

2
Layer solid items in middle.

3
Fold top and bottom edges of tortilla to center.

4
Grab left edge of tortilla and fold over inside mixture.

5
Tuck in and roll tightly to right side.

6
Heat burrito in pan on low heat to seal edges.

How to Roll Dough

1
Spread a handful of flour on clean surface.

2
Lay dough on surface.

3
Use a round object to roll dough to left.

4
Roll to right.

5
Roll up.

6
Roll down.

7
Repeat till desired thickness is reached.

How to Roll Spring Rolls

1

Run both sides of rice paper under water.

2

Layer stuffing in middle of rice paper.

3

Fold top and bottom edges to center.

4

Fold left edge to center.

5

Tuck in and roll tightly to right side.

6

Seal edge with water.

How to Roll Sushi

1

Spread rice in center of rough side of nori.

2

Layer veggies in middle of rice.

3

Grab left side and roll nori over first veggie.

4

Roll tightly to opposite side.

5

Seal edge with water.

6

Slice.

How to Shape Samosas

1

Cut dough into 3" x 3" squares.

2

Fold 2 corners inward to form a cone.

3

Spoon mixture into bottom of cone.

4

Fold open end closed.

5

Press edges together to seal in mixture.

How to Cook Grains

1
Rinse and drain grains.

2
Boil amount of water listed to right for your grain.

3
Mix in grains and a sprinkling of salt.

4
Turn heat to low, cover, and cook for time listed to right.

5
Drain any extra liquid.

Tip

- Replace water with veggie broth for more flavor.

Barley (Pearled)
Ratio: 1 cup barley to 3 cups water
Cooking Time: 30–40 min.
Makes: 3½ cups cooked

Brown Rice
Ratio: 1 cup rice to 2 cups water
Cooking Time: 30–40 min.
Makes: 3 cups cooked

Couscous
Ratio: 1 cup couscous to 1¼ cups water
Cooking Time: 5–10 min.
Makes: 2 cups cooked

Quinoa
Ratio: 1 cup quinoa to 2 cups water
Cooking Time: 15–20 min.
Makes: 3 cups cooked

Rolled Oats
Ratio: 1 cup oats to 2 cups water
Cooking Time: 20 min.
Makes: 2 cups cooked

Steel-Cut Oats
Ratio: 1 cup oats to 4 cups water
Cooking Time: 20–30 min.
Makes: 3½ cups cooked

White Rice
Ratio: 1 cup rice to 2 cups water
Cooking Time: 15–20 min.
Makes: 3 cups cooked

Wild Rice
Ratio: 1 cup rice to 3 cups water
Cooking Time: 45 min.–1 hour
Makes: 4 cups cooked

How to Cook Legumes

1
Rinse legumes in water.

2
Put legumes in a pot with 3 times as much water.

3
Bring to a boil, then remove from heat.

4
Cover and let stand for 2 to 3 hours.

5
Drain.

6
Add legumes to a pot with amount of water listed to right.

7
Cover and cook on low heat for time listed to right.

Black Beans
Ratio: 1 cup beans to 4 cups water
Cooking Time: 60–90 min.
Makes: 2¼ cups cooked

Black-Eyed Peas
Ratio: 1 cup peas to 3 cups water
Cooking Time: 60 min.
Makes: 2 cups cooked

Chickpeas (Garbanzo Beans)
Ratio: 1 cup beans to 4 cups water
Cooking Time: 1–2 hours
Makes: 2 cups cooked

Green Split Peas
Ratio: 1 cup split peas to 4 cups water
Cooking Time: 45 min.
Makes: 2 cups cooked

Kidney Beans
Ratio: 1 cup beans to 3 cups water
Cooking Time: 1 hour
Makes: 2¼ cups cooked

Lentils (Brown)
Skip steps 2–4
Ratio: 1 cup lentils to 2¼ cups water
Cooking Time: 45–60 min.
Makes: 2¼ cups cooked

Lentils (French)
Skip steps 2–4
Ratio: 1 cup lentils to 2 cups water
Cooking Time: 30–45 min.
Makes: 2 cups cooked

Lentils (Red)
Skip steps 2–4
Ratio: 1 cup lentils to 3 cups water
Cooking Time: 20–30 min.
Makes: 2 cups cooked

Lima Beans
Ratio: 1 cup beans to 4 cups water
Cooking Time: 1 hour
Makes: 2 cups cooked

Pinto Beans
Ratio: 1 cup beans to 3 cups water
Cooking Time: 1–2 hours.
Makes: 2½ cups cooked

Soybeans
Ratio: 1 cup beans to 4 cups water
Cooking Time: 3–4 hours
Makes: 3 cups cooked

White Beans (Cannellini)
Ratio: 1 cup beans to 3 cups water
Cooking Time: 45 min.
Makes: 2½ cups cooked

Index

Volume

U.S.	Imperial	Metric
1 tablespoon	½ fl oz	15 ml
2 tablespoons	1 fl oz	30 ml
¼ cup	2 fl oz	60 ml
⅓ cup	3 fl oz	90 ml
½ cup	4 fl oz	120 ml
⅔ cup	5 fl oz (¼ pint)	150 ml
¾ cup	6 fl oz	180 ml
1 cup	8 fl oz (⅓ pint)	240 ml
1¼ cups	10 fl oz (½ pint)	300 ml
2 cups (1 pint)	16 fl oz (⅔ pint)	480 ml
2½ cups	20 fl oz (1 pint)	600 ml
1 quart	32 fl oz (1⅔ pints)	1 l

Temperature

Fahrenheit	Celsius/Gas Mark
250°F	120°C/gas mark ½
275°F	135°C/gas mark 1
300°F	150°C/gas mark 2
325°F	160°C/gas mark 3
350°F	180 or 175°C/gas mark 4
375°F	190°C/gas mark 5
400°F	200°C/gas mark 6
425°F	220°C/gas mark 7
450°F	230°C/gas mark 8
475°F	245°C/gas mark 9
500°F	260°C

Length

Inch	Metric
¼ inch	6 mm
½ inch	1.25 cm
¾ inch	2 cm
1 inch	2.5 cm
6 inches (½ foot)	15 cm
12 inches	30 cm

Weight

U.S./Imperial	Metric
½ oz	15 g
1 oz	30 g
2 oz	60 g
¼ lb	115 g
⅓ lb	150 g
½ lb	225 g
¾ lb	350 g
1 lb	450 g

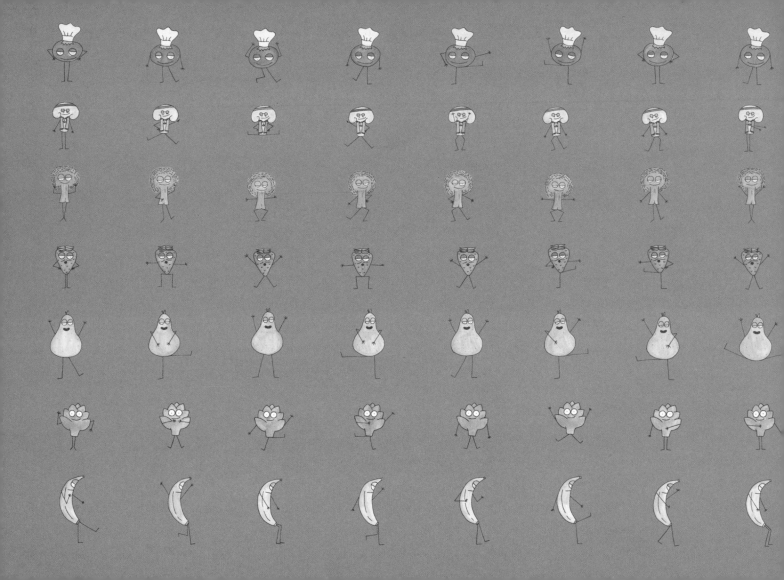